Optimize This:

How Two Carpet Cleaners Consistently Beat Web Designers On The Search Engines

Robert Anspach

Paul Douglas

Optimize This:

How Two Carpet Cleaners Consistently Beat Web Designers On The Search Engines

Optimize This:

How Two Carpet Cleaners Consistently
Beat Web Designers On The Search Engines

Published by Anspach Media
P.O. Box 2
Conestoga PA 17516

Copyright ©2014 Robert Anspach, Paul Douglas
Revised & Updated 2018

All rights reserved. No part of this book may be reproduced or transmitted in any form or by any means without the permission from the publisher.

ISBN 10: 0989466310
ISBN 13: 978-0-9894663-1-8

While they have made every effort to verify the information provided in this publication, neither the author(s) nor the publisher assumes any responsibility for errors in, omissions from or different interpretation of the subject matter.

The information herein may be subject to varying laws and practices in different areas, states and countries. The reader assumes all responsibility for use of the information.

Dedicated

To our wives...for putting up with us!

Contents

Introduction	11
Chapter 1 - What Is SEO	17
Chapter 2 - SEO Isn't Rocket Science	25
Chapter 3 - Go APE	37
Chapter 4 - The Perfect Keywords	47
Chapter 5 - Days Of Keyword Stuffing Are Over	55
Chapter 6 - Backlinks & More	63
Chapter 7 - Misconceptions Challenged	75
Chapter 8 - SEO Deconstructed	83
Chapter 9 - Optimizing YouTube	89
Chapter 10 - Getting On Page 1	97
Almost The End	105
Frequently Asked Questions	107
Glossary Of SEO Terms	111
Resources	113
Connecting With The Authors	115
Coaching Programs	116
Special Offer	117
Other Books	119

Anspach / Douglas

Introduction

My cohort and I have a combined lifetime of cleaning up after people. First in the carpet cleaning industry and now as SEO cleaners. Oops, did I say "cleaners"? I meant bullies. (You'll see why soon). And yes, the cleaning up part is still true. We clean up the messes the web designers make on others' websites. Ironically, neither one of us knew that 15 years ago our paths would cross outside carpet cleaning forums, nor that we would transition from owners of carpet cleaning companies to sought after SEO experts.

Both of us, learning from the same marketing masters started taking the concepts taught to us to rapidly grow our cleaning operations with high end customers. It was the beginning of our process. Discovering how certain words compel people to trust you, buy from you, and refer you to others.

And, as you'll discover throughout this book, we both tackled the mess and frustration that having a web designer with no SEO skills brought us. We took matters into our own hands and crudely made our own websites. Over the course of a dozen years we perfected our skill sets. We stumbled like many, but before long we were the dominant ranking websites in our markets.

Others started to notice. "Hey, how come you rank on page 1 of Google and I don't?" was the typical question. That was all it took to open the doors to a conversation. Then a job optimizing a website, then another...and before long we were the "go-to" guys in our areas.

What you'll discover in this book is quite simply time tested proven ideas, concepts and strategies that will enhance your website ranking and get you on or close to page 1 on the various search engines. None of it is trickery. In fact, as much as we hate to say it...it's basic common sense stuff.

But, but, but, but...what about Google's algorithms? Yeah, you'll soon realize that although we show people how to "magically" rank on page 1, we are not fans of how they name their updates after smelly animals. Follow the concepts we lay out and get rewarded by Google updates instead of slapped. Finally, you'll come across a few places where we downright dispel the myths and misconceptions of what web designers are saying you must have for your website.

Geek speak makes it sound so confusing, but honestly, it comes down to knowing what works and how to apply it. It is as simple as that. No rocket science required. No sacrificing virgins on the search engine altars. It is our hope that we made this book not so technical that you get frustrated, but easy enough that you'll say...wow, those guys are brilliant.

Yep, two former carpet cleaners changing the way SEO is done. Who'd a thunk it?

Now, with this book in hand, you my friend, have the ability to change the way your website is ranked. Follow the advice we share and you could even become the next SEO bully. Again we mention "bully"...and, shortly you'll discover what that means and why it's important to be one.

And yes, we encourage you to write to us, and tell us how this book helped you. Or hire us and let us do the work for you.

But first, we'd like to share with you a little bit more about us...

Robert "Rob" **Anspach**, a native of Lancaster County PA, started in the carpet cleaning field in 1993. In the winter of 1995 he opened Premiere Carpet Cleaners and for three years struggled. By 1998, desperate and almost dead broke, Rob took a chance on a marketing seminar in Phoenix, Arizona that quickly and miraculously saved his butt. Well, sort of. Rob put into action all the marketing knowledge he gleaned from the seminar to rapidly grow his carpet cleaning business, and so, saved his own butt.

Rob started crafting his own ads, fliers, sales letters and marketing materials to gain high-end, premium clients. By 2001, Rob was teaching the concepts to other cleaners. It was during this time Rob discovered that certain keywords had different effects ranking websites and after tweaking his website for the umpteenth time, got it to rank on Page 1 of Google. Twelve years later, it was still on page 1.

In 2009, Rob started teaching social media to cleaners and other entrepreneurs so they could use this new-fangled way of communicating with others as a way to build trust and gain new sales. Four years later Rob authored two books, "*Social Media Debunked*", and "*Share: 27 Ways to Boost Your Social Media Experience, Build Trust and Attract Followers*".

Rob still lives in Lancaster County with his wife Kim, their six children, one grandchild and a noisy beagle named Buddy.

Paul Douglas, like Rob, spent over twenty years as a carpet cleaner, eleven of which was as the owner of Douglas Home Cleaning. It was during this period that Paul discovered direct response marketing and had his first website built.

Paul used the training he had in direct response and applied it to his website. As a result, he stumbled across the secret to ranking on the top of the search engines.

That secret will be revealed inside this book.

After retiring from carpet cleaning, Paul tried to return to the work force, but the allure of internet marketing and the lifestyle it promised, was like a siren song calling out for his credit card number. It wasn't long before local business owners asked Paul to develop their websites.

A local protective coatings company hired Paul as their marketing director. In six months, using the practices shared in this book, his employer was on literally the first fifteen pages of Google, with the first competitor showing up on page seven and the second on page fifteen. He became the search engine bully that pushed every competitor into obscurity.

With a very powerful and compelling case study in hand, Paul launched Titan Marketing Solutions in 2012 with the goal of helping all his clients get found on all online platforms, on every connected device, in every desk, lap, pocket and purse.

Paul still lives in his hometown of Winnipeg with his wife and partner Lisa, with her daughter, their two dogs Le Hardi and Penny as well as their cat, Jack.

Wonder Twin powers activate! Hah, okay we are not twins. But we both have a love of helping entrepreneurs grow their businesses through effective keywords and content. And it's those keywords and content, regardless of whether in print form or online that will continue to provide sales to businesses. This book helps guide you through the online process and allows you to understand the dynamics of using proper keywords and content to boost your search engine optimization.

    Enjoy

Chapter 1

What is SEO?

If someone had asked me to turn on a computer I would have turned off the lights, lit some candles, played soft music, poured a glass of wine and whispered to the computer, "I love you."

In a nutshell, SEO is anything you can do to get your website to rank higher on the various search engines for the keywords and content that reflect your industry. SEO is an acronym which stands for Search Engine Optimization.

The biggest takeaway you'll get from this chapter is the fact that contrary to popular belief, SEO is not dead. It is still very much required to get your website to rank higher on the search engines. Oh, yeah...it's most definitely required.

You see, optimizing a website is by far the best way to get people to find you when searching for what you do or how you can help them. But it's full of myths, confusion, misdirection and down-right lies.

Yes, it's true search engine optimization helps your website rank higher using effective keywords and content...but its main purpose is to create added traffic to your website and then added sales and profits for your business. The most effective way we know how to do that is to displace your competitors' listings with yours. Essentially, you want to bully them off the front page by kicking your competitors out of the proverbial search engine sandbox and stealing their lunch money.

There we said it.

There is no taking it back. The ultimate goal of SEO is to make you the dominant player in your field so when consumers are searching for you, the only choice they see is you. Yep, you bully your competitors right off of page one...and then *you* dominate the market.

But, we digress...and we're getting ahead of ourselves here.

So, let's take a step back.

We're going to cover a lot of things in this book. You're going to learn the difference between Search Engine Optimization and Search Engine Marketing. And yes, they are two different animals. Web designers seem to throw the terms out loosely and I have come to the conclusion that most have no idea what the difference is.

True SEO is the "on page" keywords and content you encode into your website that tells the consumer and the search engines your site is worthy of Page One status. SEM (Search Engine Marketing) is how you position "off page" keywords and content to help push your website higher on the search engines. (More on that in a later chapter.) Don't confuse Search Engine Marketing with paid search. When you pay for a position on the search engine results page, that is advertising.

Search Engine Optimization needs to be the focus that you take when you think about what your website is supposed to be…you know…how does it reflect your business…how does it get your message out there to your ideal customer?

There's a lot of beautiful websites out there, but they're never going to be seen because they're not optimized with keywords and content to get the search engines to know they exist. It is like placing a great big huge billboard at the end of a dead end street no one ever drives down. It is not visible, therefore it is not creating sales for your business, and subsequently that beautiful website you are so proud of has become a colossal waste of money.

So the prime focus is going to be Search Engine Optimization, and really, it's taking those key words and content and making sure that your site shows up somewhere on Google, preferably on the first page.

But wait...

It's not just getting your website on the first page, it's getting multiple pages of your website on page one and squeezing out your competitors.

Early Days - Paul

The rules, like so many things, have changed. It was so easy ten years ago to put up a website and throw on a bunch of relevant key words; stuff them all over the place and you will get it ranked.

Case in point, the first website that I built was in 2003 and it was for my carpeting cleaning business, Douglas Home Cleaning. Now I was absolutely clueless at the time about building a website and I was also clueless about how to write code.

As a matter of fact, a couple of years before that, if someone had asked me to turn on a computer I would have turned off the lights, lit some candles, played soft music, poured a glass of wine and whispered to the computer, "I love you."

I say that to show you how technically incompetent I was at the time. So my first website was already pretty much built for me. All I had to do was go in, edit and modify the content.

So when I went in and edited the content I changed it, then customized it for my carpet cleaning business. I took the training and knowledge that I received from Joe Polish and other Direct Response Marketers and I used a lot of copy and content for my website and that's how I kind of stumbled across the secrets that we are going to be covering in the book.

Early Days - Rob

Well, you know both of us came from the same industry... carpet cleaning. I had been in the cleaning industry since 1993. By 2013 I thought it was time...time to get out. I did what I set out to do and discovered how to create brilliant marketing along the way. I learned how to do SEO because, as the owner of a small company, my resources were limited and my faith in others diminished.

In 1996, I hired a web designer to create this beautiful site for my carpet cleaning business and it was just there in the "void" not being seen by anyone. And there I am scratching my head wondering why I just spent two thousand dollars for nothing.

The following year I took the site down and thought, you know what, I am going to do this myself. I had really no experience with HTML but I learned and I made this long sales letter type website which was the rage back then. The problem with these long websites now is that they don't rank.

Back then I had that particular site so filled with key words, so filled with why you need to buy from me, that it stayed ranked for a good ten years.

The problem was that I had all that content on one page and there is no way to optimize it to be effective. So my best bet was to take all that content that I had and spread it out over five to ten pages.

Now the fun part...

Here's how SEO truly works.

Now you have shorter content on each page and it's a lot easier to optimize each page. So it compliments, but competes with the main page to spread your message across Google and the other search engines to get your site ranked faster.

And here's the trick. If you have this long sales page like Rob had and someone was looking for "upholstery cleaning in Lancaster", but your first page was optimized for carpet cleaning, they are never going to find you and this is the mistake we see that a lot of people are making.

You are optimizing that first page thinking, "Wow that's all I need", and then they look at the second page, the third page, the fourth page, and there is nothing.

So if the consumer is looking for that upholstery cleaner who happens to be set up on, let's say, a tab on your third page, they are never going to find it because it's not optimized.

Now every page needs to be optimized for the keywords and content on that page. If you have carpet cleaning on one page, upholstery on another page, tile cleaning...we think you get the idea, each keyword now is a separate page that can rank better just for itself. And so, when I took my long form website and broke it down into ten pages my site just exploded and people were finding me for services that they never found me for before.

There is so much you can do now with a website you couldn't do a couple of years ago but people are still stuck on these old websites that really are just nothing more than an electronic billboard. You need to have a blog on that website and videos and fresh content.

Oh, yes...fresh content.

Fresh content on a consistent basis lets Google and the other search engines know that your website is still active.

The big problem we see is the owner of these sites are just letting them be abandoned and they are not putting content up, not editing it, not changing it, not doing anything to it. They just say, "Well, here is my money, just let the site go up there and we will see what it does for us", and that is the wrong approach to website design, and it is the wrong approach to thinking that your sites are going to do anything for you.

To be honest, if that's your approach, don't put a website up at all, because honestly you're just throwing your money away. Get that site built so that it is tracking the right type of clients with the right key words with the right content and that site will make you money.

Do you want to be part of the noise or control the noise?

The Simple Explanation...

Back in the early 1970's the average person experienced roughly 500 advertising messages a day. By the 1990's that number had jumped to 5,000 and today (2014) the number of advertising messages we see on a daily basis is close to 13,000.

The point is, there is a lot of noise out there and we are all screaming for a customer's attention. Yeah, a lot of noise.

That's what search engines are designed to do, give us relevant answers without the noise. We type in keywords or phrases and hope the search engines with their infinite wisdom spit out the answers to our questions.

Relevant answers! Seems simple, right?

That's the quandary of SEO!

As we proceed through this book you'll discover how to select the right keywords and phrases that are relevant and that ultimately get the consumer to make a purchase.

The reality is this...make sure that you optimize. And do it without industry jargon! Make it simple and easy for your audience to understand what your message is and what you are trying to communicate.

Chapter 2
SEO Isn't Rocket Science

It's all about the money!

Years ago, when you wanted to search for a contractor you would have flipped open a phonebook, looked for the industry that best represented that service and find the one that matched your inquiry. Generations of people did it this way. Now those days are gone. Phonebooks have become obsolete.

This was brought home to me just a few years ago. I had attended a morning breakfast meeting at a local BNI chapter as an alternate for my chiropractor. When the meeting was over, my vehicle, was not where I parked it. Turns out, I was running late and mistakenly parked in a no parking zone.

I was driven home by one of the members of this BNI group. The first thing I did was pick up the phonebook. Now maybe it was cost savings on the part of the phone company, or my eyes were 43 years old, but I couldn't read the listings. It was all blurry.

I closed the phone book in frustration, turned on the computer (no soft music required at this point), opened up Google and searched for the towing company and their phone number. It came up in seconds, I made a call and then got a ride down to their compound to recover my vehicle. Since then, I have used phonebooks as door stops.

Let's face it. It is not just me. Now it's all Bing this, Google that! Searches have been reduced to mere seconds. The results can be confusing and not exactly fruitful.

Try searching for "*Dallas kitchen contractor*" and Google will return 4,110,000 results. Who has time to search through 4 million listings? Bring back the phone book please. It wasn't as fast but only had a few hundred choices, not the millions that were displayed through Google.

It's not just a problem for the consumer trying to find the right "*Dallas kitchen contractor*", it's also a problem for the "*Dallas Kitchen Contractor*" to get noticed. Or in the search engines case to get that "*Dallas Kitchen Contractor*" listed on page 1 of the results. Because just like phone books, people gravitate to the ads on the first few pages; it's the same for Google, Bing, Yahoo and the rest of the many search engines out there. Four million results? No way! Most people don't go past the first page of Google, that's why it's very important to get your listing keyworded just right.

If you're the "*Dallas Kitchen Contractor*" who is listed in those 4 million results unless you are on page 1, sadly, your odds of getting your website noticed equates to being the proverbial needle in a haystack.

But there is hope.

Both consumers and contractors alike can reduce the search time and narrow down the choices by keywording their inquiries into longer phrases that give a better understanding of exactly what they need. So instead of *"Dallas Kitchen Contractor"* which displays way too many listings try *"Dallas Kitchen and Bath Contractor"*. Well okay maybe not, but it did reduce the results in half. But, honestly 2 million is still way too many.

"Dallas Custom Kitchen and Bath Contractor" returned 1.7 million results. Yet if I use the term *"Fort Worth Custom Kitchen and Bath Contractor"* the results are reduced dramatically down to 256,000. Now that's a big difference. When you add *"Licensed"* in front of your *"Fort Worth Custom Kitchen and Bath Contractor"* inquiry, you cut the results further in half.

Here's the trick to getting better search results and reducing the amount of time required to wade through the sea of endless listings. Use the names of smaller towns around you first. If you live in Dallas or Fort Worth the results of your search will be cumbersome. Yet, if you use the towns in between like *"Arlington"*, *"Grapevine"*, *"Grand Prairie"* or even *"Hurst"* instead of *"Dallas"* or *"Fort Worth"* your results will be far superior and you'll reduce your time searching.

The right keywords can make or break a search. It's those keywords that Google and the other search engines look at that determine your results.

All these keywords are actually part of a system that the search engines use to classify and specify the results of searches. This is how SEO works! SEO stands for Search Engine Optimization. It actually means that the websites being listed have been optimized for web searches. So those sites pulling up on page 1 of Google most likely have been keyworded in such a way as to attract the right searches.

Being specific, using long phrases, in your searches actually gains the best results. Using general terms like "*Dallas Contractor*" and you'll be spending weeks wading through the 12 million results you receive.

*The more specific you are,
the better results you'll receive.*

SEO is not rocket science, it just takes a little understanding of what words people are using. If you can master the words, then your results will stand out.

Consumers benefit by getting the right results. Contractors benefit by getting new and wonderful clients. The right keywords make all the difference. And yes, it works for any town, any industry, anywhere! Words can change lives...or in this case...match consumers with contractors. And to some, having a remodeled kitchen or bath is a life changing event.

Life changing events start with getting slapped sometimes!

Here's Paul to shed some light on the slapping and what he did to help guide a client to get back to their top of page one ranking.

You know a lot of times so many people will say with all these Google updates that are out there that they are getting slapped, getting delisted, moving down, getting hurt by these updates. I'd like to share a story of one of the sites that I created about 5 years ago. It was for a local manufacturer of vending machines and with everything that I was doing to get him set up he was always very solid on page two page or three. In spite of all the effort, all the videos and everything else that we did.

But, an amazing thing happened about 3 years ago when there was this smelly little animal from Google called Panda came out. Panda was their search engine algorithm update. Many competitors websites were ahead of my client. They were older sites, had more authority (because of their age) and some of the things that they had done got moved down or even delisted as a result of this Panda update and my client's site is now ranking quite well in the search engines as a result of these updates .

Here's why...

Search engines want to end search. Essentially, what they do is when you go to Google or any other search engine for that matter, if you take a look along the top and along the side of that search engine result page (or SERP as we call it), you're going to see ads. It's these ads that you see on the search engine results page and everywhere else on the internet that pays Google's bills and makes them the profitable company that they are.

So what they want to do is create a unique and exceptional user experience for you, the Google user. So when you go to Google what they want you to do is search for something.

They want to give you high quality results so when you click on one of the results that they have listed on that page from one to 10 that your question gets answered. Back to relevancy!

It's really about creating content for the end user... the consumer.

Don't try to game the system, or trick the search engine spiders.

If you're new to the world of SEO, a search engine

spider is basically a program the various search engines use to crawl through and index all the sites and information on the world wide web.

Your website is not there to please search engine spiders. So, the first and foremost rule when it comes to content on a website is to write for the person or the individual or your ideal customer that is going to be coming to your website. RELEVANCY!

Your website is there to create business for (or sales for) your business, whether it be through leads or actual sales. Your website is there to make you money.

Write for the person you're wanting to attract to your website because...bottom line, search engine spiders are not going to buy your product or service.

So when you write your copy for your content it should be in a way that reflects how somebody's going to read it.

And if you make it too technical, or if you make it too industry heavy...it'll tell Google, "hey you know this website is just stuffed full of keywords". Google might just then push your site down the ranks because it's not consumer friendly. Your website content needs a healthy balance between consumer friendly and industry standard words to make it work better.

But I want that particular keyword to rank...

Well, okay that's great, but if that keyword is not mentioned anywhere on the pages of your website it has no relevance.

There are a couple of examples that I like to share talking about relevance on a webpage.

There was an individual that had asked me to do a half day consulting with him for his website some time ago. He was a local photographer. He actually had listed on his webpage that he did wedding photography, wedding videography, portrait photography, business photography and aerial photography.

Now, he had all five lines of business on his homepage. Which, ok, I can accept that as far as keywords but then every page also had the exact same keywords. A total UGH!

Now I don't know about you but I think aerial photography is nowhere near relevant to wedding photography and vice versa.

Relevancy wasn't as much of a big deal four or five years ago when I did his initial consultation but definitely now the way the rules have changed, especially with all of Google's updates. Now, if you're not relevant from the title to the description, to the keywords to the content on the page, you're not going to rank. Even five years ago, I saw people suffering because of the lack of relevance and consistency on their webpage.

Rocket science? Not even close!

Relevance! That's what it's all about. Oh, and proper keywords and content.

That's one of the key things. Content is going to win. It's always going to win.

That was something I discovered in 2003 when I built my carpet cleaning business. I ranked very well because I put my content in it. My first website after I retired from carpet cleaning was for a print broker. And it ranked very well because of the relevance of the content.

I will be quite honest. I had no clue as to what I was doing. I just did what I thought was normal and natural and had to be done to pass my best job to the end user. I wasn't thinking about pleasing search engine spiders. I had no clue what search engine spiders were at that time except critters that would scare my girlfriend. So I didn't write for the search engines. I wrote because I wanted to sell carpet cleaning and I wrote because I wanted to sell printing.

Yep, Paul got it. And so can you. It's not rocket science! It's so much more.

Speaking of more...let's talk about pictures.

Yes, those picture on your website.

Are they relevant?

Is the picture labeled correctly or was it "borrowed" (swiped, garnered, stolen) from someone else's site?

Let's examine why labeling is important to boosting SEO and making your site relevant to page rank.

Using a photo straight from its source (digital camera, smart phone, tablet, etc.) gives you a description of the image that's really not appealing (example: G275354329091.jpeg). Before you embed that image (or upload that picture) to your website it's best to rename the image to something that best describes the relevance to your industry.

So instead of "G275354329091.jpeg" if being from the carpet cleaning industry the new description could be "carpet-cleaning-albuquerque-residential.jpeg".

Just name the image something that is relevant to your industry.

Now about that "borrowed" thing.

Coming from the carpet cleaning industry we see ads out there with the same photograph in all of them.

Super cleaning guy!

Thousands of cleaning companies using this one guy in all of their ads, websites and marketing. And no, there is no super cleaning model and no, he did not pose for all these carpet cleaning companies.

Can you say "stock photo"?

I am sorry but if you're going to share a stock photo...don't!

Stock photos are great for some things but for originality, for content authority and for search engine ranking...stock photos are awful. But hey, everyone is doing it!

Yeah, okay...**NO!**

If you are serious about dominating the search engines than be unique! Have original content!

Don't borrow, swipe or downright steal others pictures or content.

It may not seem like a big deal…but others have gone to great lengths to capture those photos or write that brilliant content. Let them have it.

Searching for and protecting your images.

- Watermark all images prior to putting them on your website (or social pages).
- Use Google Search or Tin Eye to scan your image to make sure others aren't using it.

Unique photos and brilliantly written copy are the keys to attracting the right clients. Yes, relevant content can make all the difference between a quantity of lookers to a quality of buyers.

FYI: A cool app to use on your smart phone to watermark your photos prior to sharing on your website or social sites is called iWatermark…check it out.

Chapter 3

Go APE!

Even Lady Gaga could learn this way!

Let's start this chapter off with a simple exercise. We want you to Google both your name and your company's name. And for this exercise, let's say you make widgets.

Did you come up on page one? Possibly at the very top? If you did, shut down your happy dance and fist pump.

Sure you're coming up on Page 1 of Google...**for your name!** But, unfortunately 99% of people searching don't know you and if they do, most likely aren't spelling your name correctly.

Your customers and prospects are looking for solutions to a problem, or to buy a product or service you provide. So they most likely searched for…

How do I fix my widget?

How do I make my widget work better?

Where can I get my widget fixed?

Where do I buy widgets?

I didn't see your name or company name anywhere in those questions.

Search queries or keywords like you see above that you place in your Meta Title along with a Meta Description (see Chapter 8 where we talk more about Meta) is what Google and the other search engines use to find and rank you. Using your name takes up valuable keyword real estate. Yes, we all like our name up top and in lights...it just feels and looks nice. But, in the SEO world...sorry to say...your name means diddly-squat.

Your name is irrelevant!

Paul and I see you shaking your head in disagreement. Okay, we can play that game.

This is how important your name really is... nada, zip, zilch! What about Trump, Lady Gaga, Coca-Cola, Apple or even Bill Gates? Surely they have name recognition?

When it comes to internet searches, even those names get misspelled, misquoted, butchered and beaten just like the rest of our names. Take any given day you receive mail, we bet one of those pieces has your name misspelled. Ours do! Or maybe you get a call from someone mispronouncing your name...doesn't that just irritate you. They couldn't even try to say your name right.

Or how about you're listening to a song and you have no clue who the performer is, or someone tells you but you don't know how to spell it. You Google it and now you're coming up with bad results. You could use the words in the song to simplify your search and increase your chances of finding the best results.

One of the first things we do when asked to audit a website for possible optimization, is look at the title banner...the header that shows up at the top of your website. Depending on the browser you're using it could be displayed in the search bar or above the search bar. This title shows what is being displayed to Google and the other search engines. Words that could impact how people search you.

Instead of using your name... may I suggest you use keywords that best describe you: NY Medical Malpractice Attorney, Las Vegas Plastic Surgeon, Lancaster PA Chocolate Maker, Albuquerque NM Carpet Cleaner. These are the terms that people use to search. They are in essence the natural way of finding what you are after...use specific keywords followed by a city and state. Yep, the use of keywords will enable people to find you when they have no clue what your name is or how to spell it. Sure, they might find your competitor, but then again, your competitors clients might find you instead.

In order to win the placement of first page ranking with Google and the other search engines it's essential your keywords are geared to what people are searching.

But what words? How do you choose?

In this chapter we peel back the process and show you how to go bananas over selecting the right keywords. In fact you're going to Go **APE** over the whole thing.

Seriously, this chapter helps explain the thinking behind keyword selection and search engine ranking.

APE is an acronym Rob coined that best reflects the thinking involved in finding the right words. Words that make the difference in ranking your website on Page 1 of Google or on Page 3475. Hey, if you're not on Page 1 then it doesn't matter where you are. Rarely do people search beyond the first page. So, it's important to know the process of key wording.

It's more than your name.

And, it's how people will find you.

APE stands for...

- **A**nalytical
- **P**sychological
- **E**motional

Analytical keywords are those that describe your industry. The terms you use every day to talk about your product or service. They are specific. They are relevant. They are in essence the way you think about your work.

Psychological keywords are those that define the types of clients you are after. How they think. How they live. Where they live. And, what they believe in. These are the keywords that help you get into their way of thinking.

Emotional keywords are words consumers will respond to faster. They are words that compel us to do something, agitate in a certain way, or motivate us to buy. These are the keywords that push peoples buttons.

Yes, it's a process.

And yes, in order to rank your website on Page 1 it requires you to do some research.

In a subsequent chapter you will discover how we research keywords by using industry bulletin boards, forums, community chat rooms and look at the words that consumers are using to talk about your product and service.

So here's a keyword exercise...

When you are trying to come up with the perfect keywords, write them all down. Yep, all of them. Hundreds of them.

Go get yourself a pen and paper tablet.

Make three columns.

Analytical, Psychological and Emotional.

When you are writing those words, what columns do you think they go in? Yes, some may fit multiple columns depending how they are used.

Write each word in the appropriate column. Don't over think it. Just write them down.

Keep jotting down words until you have at least 25 in each column.

Now repeat this process for every page on your website.

Stop shaking your head and just do it.

You want to rank right? Well this is how you get your keywords to work for you.

Do this for every page that you have on your website. If you have 10 products, each product needs its own page, every page needs to have its own set of keywords.

This goes back to the "***your name is irrelevant***" part.

Using proper keywords to search for someone allows you to pinpoint exactly what you are looking for without guessing.

We have seen many websites that people are using

the same keywords, the same title, the same description for every single page. None of the pages are ranking because it's duplicated, and to Google's magical web crawling spider bots they see your duplicate keywords as redundant and not worthy of listing.

Every page needs to be unique, has to have relevant content and has to have keywords that tell Google and the consumers why it's important to go to that page.

Using **APE** style keywords helps attract the right clients into your search result funnel while eliminating the window shopper "no money" customers. Honestly, most web designers make websites that are geared to attracting anyone who can breathe...and, sadly that's a bad business model and wastes your time and those that are only looking for a low cost deal.

If we're sitting down with, for instance, a massage therapist or a chiropractor or a dentist or anybody that's not in the cleaning field and is new to us, we need to know everything there is to know about their field. Not only are we going to ask them a lot of questions which they are going to probably tell us more of the analytical side, we're going to do research. We're going to go on the internet, to different types of places, to find out what drives people to wanting to use that service. That process is mainly overlooked in a lot of the development of websites.

You need to have more of the compelling aspect to

your site.

Okay, now that you've selected a few keywords and phrases to use in your Meta Title and Description...here's a trick to get people to call you.

Put your phone number either in the title or the description of the page. Because, sometimes people are on their smartphones, or they are in their workplace and they don't have time to look at your website but they do have time to click on that phone number and call you. Now you are coming up not only on page 1, beating out your competitors, but your phone number is right there. They can call you without going to your website. I know that's kind of counterproductive, we want them to go to the website but the main thing is we want them to pick up that phone, to call, to place an order, to buy your product or to ask questions.

Go **APE** with a phone number...hmm, how interesting. Yep, you can say that. But are you going to do it?

Remember the story Paul shared in the previous chapter? The one where he parked illegally and got his car towed?

Paul used Google the way it was designed to be used...finding a service using keywords, then calling that service with questions. In this case that question was…

"Do you have my car?"

If you put your phone number in the description, particularly if it's in the first 156 characters of that description, it's going to show up in the search engines results. And it will enable those searching for you a faster way to gain access to you with questions or concerns.

One caveat...when inserting your phone number into your description (or placing on your website) use dashes not dots.

Option 1 – **(215)123-0000** - YES

Option 2 – **215-123-0000** - YES

Option 3 – **215.123.0000** - NO

A phone number with dots may look nice and artsy-fartsy but the search engines will confuse it with an ISP address and if you try to click on it, you may be diverted to some unknown nether region of the interwebs. Not fun. So use Option 1 or 2 and if thinking about using Option 3...just forget it.

Chapter 4

The Perfect Keywords

Searching for words in all the right places.

In this chapter, we're going to be talking about probably the most important and yet, most underutilized part of SEO. That is, finding the exact keywords that your customers are using to find you online. Keyword research is vitally important, whether you're going to be doing a campaign for a paid search or just to position your website so that you're in front of your customers when they are looking for you.

Before that though, just a quick question. Where do you go to find the keywords that you optimize for your sites?

If Rob is keywording for a medical malpractice attorney in New York, he's going to search medical malpractice forums, bulletin boards, and things that consumers will actually type. Then he'll combine it with industry language that the lawyers might use to get a better idea of the keywords that best represents their needs. Then Rob will go into Google Trends and see if people are using those specific words. If they're not, then it's kind of pointless to SEO a site with words that aren't being used. By utilizing words that are actually being searched, we can guarantee a better, higher ranking on Google, Bing, and Yahoo.

Paul's take is a little different...a more traditionalist approach.

Typically what Paul will do is start off with what everyone else does. That's where the similarity ends.

It goes like this...

First, go to AdWords.Google.com.

Now you do need to have an AdWords account to login, but it doesn't cost anything to setup an account until you actually use it in a campaign. AdWords gives you access to their keyword research.

The thing you have to remember with the keyword tool from Google is that these are keywords that other businesses are bidding on. It doesn't necessarily mean this is what people are clicking on. It's just what other businesses are bidding on. But it's a good place to start, just to give you an idea, if nothing else, just some of the long-tailed keywords in your industry that might be available to you that you haven't thought of.

The second thing Paul likes to do once he's compiled that list is researching through Google Trends. You can research five keywords at a time at Google Trends, and you can see the history of the search on a particular keyword. You can see how many people in your area are searching that particular keyword. Is it going up? Is it going down? Has it flat lined? It's a very valuable tool.

A couple of the other things that Paul likes to do is using Google's auto-suggest tool. It's a drop down from the search bar. The auto-suggest feature gives search terms that people are currently using right now in real-time.

Example: Type "*used cars Winnipeg*" into your search bar. Use the auto-suggest feature.

If Paul does the search based on his location his Google auto-suggests might display...

"*used cars Winnipeg under 2000*"

"*used cars Winnipeg dealers*"

"*used cars Winnipeg under 3000*"

Now, if I'm a used car dealer and I've got vehicles under 2000 and 3000 dollars, that might be a keyword that I would want to put in. Of course, "*used cars Winnipeg dealer*", is definitely something that just about every dealer in the city's going to bid on, so that's going to be a highly competitive keyword.

FYI: if you go to the bottom of that search page, you're going to have searches that are related to your keyword.

Searches that are related to "*used cars Winnipeg*" could be:

"*used car dealers Winnipeg*"

"*used cars Winnipeg under 5000*"

"*Autotrader*" - now that's a branded auto publication

"*used cars Winnipeg private sale*"

When Rob does that same search using the auto-suggest tool, "*used cars Winnipeg*", from his home state of Pennsylvania, Google spits out slightly different results. The result was "*used cars Winnipeg bad credit*". That could be a term those with not-so-great credit use to search for cars.

Now, let's expand it a bit further.

Paul has "*used cars under 2000*", and wants to expand to "*used cars Winnipeg under 10,000*". If people are looking for cars under a price range, they've set their budget. By covering a price range you are thinking like a consumer and honing in on words that appeal to the masses. Do you think that's a buying keyword? They've set their budget. They want a vehicle that doesn't cost them more than a set amount.

Just by doing this exercise, you've come up with a keyword strategy that you can start implementing for yourself right now. Or for a client if you want to make SEO your career. You can do the related searches, but don't be afraid to use the auto-suggest from Google as well.

People confuse ranking one word versus multi-words or a phrase. Your best bet is to always rank for multi-words, as we just explained this being "***used cars Winnipeg***". That's a phrase. That's something that people should rank for because, if they just said "***used cars***", they might be in competition with a million different listings. If they have more of a phrase that they're ranking for they're going to get a better type of consumer looking for them.

If you're a local business, why are you going to rank for a keyword that may be global in search, and compete on a global scale. If you're a used car dealer in Pennsylvania and you sell a car to somebody in Manitoba, great. More power to you, but that's few and far between type of thing that in most cases won't happen, frequently...if ever. And, we honestly think you're going to be more interested in selling cars in your own backyard, to customers in your immediate area. Knowing your geographical limits is always good too. It'll make your search results so much more relevant.

Again, keyword research is very vital.

It's something that most people spend very little time on, and it is probably the most important step in the entire search engine optimization process. Let's face it, you come up with an obscure keyword that nobody ever looks for - easy to rank for it. Who cares if you're number 1 or even number 1 to 150 for it. If nobody's searching for it, what does it matter where it ranks?

If you're doing keyword research, search your keyword. One of the other indicators as far as the power of that keyword, is how many people are bidding on that in the ads. If you do a search on a keyword and there are no ads, then it's not a buying keyword. If nobody's trying to rank for that keyword with the Google AdWords tool, then it's not getting searched enough for people to want to advertise it.

As you maneuver each keyword in and out of Google AdWords and see the cost involved of selecting those keywords if you decide to use it as a paid campaign and run ads. If you can actually rank for those keywords organically, you won't have to pay AdWords any money to do so.

Hey, if nothing else, you can use that as a way to justify your budget, or even set a budget if you hire an SEO consultant. If you know that each click for a specific keyword is going to cost you, say 12 dollars for each click that you get to your site using an AdWords campaign then, you know that if you get, say a thousand clicks from your SEO consultant for that same keyword, that's 12,000 dollars' worth of traffic that your SEO consultant just gave you. If his fee is less than that 12,000 dollars, then you're definitely ahead of the game.

The point we are saying is one of the benefits of search engine optimization, is that unlike AdWords, your results... will always maintain itself. It's not going to disappear when your budget runs out. It's going to continue to work for you long after you pay a consultant.

Whereas AdWords will only stay for as long as you continue to pay Google. Whether you're using paid search or on-page optimization, if you don't start by using the keywords that people are searching for, then you're throwing your time and money down the drain.

FYI: The keywords that you're selecting need to be relevant for the pages that you want to rank for. Let's say page 2 on your website has certain content; the keywords that you want to represent need to match that content. We've seen so many AdWords campaigns use the wrong keywords, and it doesn't correlate to anything that's on that page. You're wasting your money and you're not attracting the clients that you had hoped will come to that page. You really need to use relevant keywords that represent what's on that page first.

Chapter 5

Days Of Keyword Stuffing Are Over

Avoiding the freefall into the chasm of oblivion.

Do you know of someone that got delisted from the search engines?

Early on in his SEO career, Rob was working with a client who came to him and asked to get an opinion on something, and Rob said, "No, I don't think that's going to work." As Rob was doing the keyword search and plugging in his keywords and getting the clients site ranked, the client went ahead and used a service being sold on Fiverr.

Fiverr has some good things, but apparently, on this particular gig, the service the client used got him delisted. They did some funky stuff that, in our opinion, was unethical. The site was delisted, and it took almost eight months for the site to come back on to Google. Then we had to go back in and clean everything up. It happens.

There are things that Paul is going to explain to you, that hopefully, will help protect you from being delisted.

It's funny, because every single day I get an email from an internet marketer that says, "Black hat is back," or get an email from an internet marketer talking about a Google loophole that you can exploit. Folks, this is why Google does all these notorious updates. Google continuously updates their search algorithms with codenames like Panda, Penguin and other smelly farm animals. Its sole purpose is to stop people who are creating poor quality content to try to elevate themselves in the search rankings artificially, creating a poor user experience for the searcher.

What we tell our clients is this...

If we were smarter than Google, we would be working for Google. Using black hat strategies or exploiting loopholes may work for a while. Eventually, it will get closed, and your search engine ranking will freefall into the chasm of oblivion.

It's a "churn and burn" marketing philosophy. If you're looking for a quick buck, if you're not looking for a long-term viable business, then by all means, use some of these tactics and keep using them. But, you're not going to create any growth or longevity out of it.

If you're like Rob and I, and the clients that we deal with, we have a long term business model. We want to grow our business, we want to be around for a long time, so you don't want to do anything that is shady, unethical, or even questionable in the eyes of the search engines.

They have their terms of service, what you can and cannot do as far as being an advertiser. If you follow the same concepts and principles when you build your site, you should be okay.

Everybody talks about black hat, white hat, grey hat. What is black hat? What is white hat? What's grey hat? What works?

Black hat would be, for lack of better words, a lot of the old school tactics. This would be where you would stuff your site full of keywords, whether they were relevant to that particular page or not. You'd just stuff them into the webpage.

When the search engines shut that idea down, people started taking those same keywords and putting them at the bottom of the page. Often times hiding them by making the color of those keywords the same color as the page itself, so it would be invisible to the visitor, but would be picked up by the search engines.

Going out and putting out irrelevant content everywhere, just with the link back from that website to your site would be another black hat technique.

Don't get me wrong, we'll cover back links in the

next chapter. They're good, they're valuable, they'll help you rank, but it's changed. I used to tell people, again, this is old school. If you've ever heard the line, "The person who dies with the most toys wins." That is very similar for search engine optimization three years ago, where the website that has the most links, wins. Now it's the website with the most relevant, high quality links that wins.

What is white hat? White hat is basically following the guidelines that is put out by Google to optimize your website, to get found. There's people out there that will follow Matt Cutts from Google, and will follow every suggestion he makes to the letter.

Does white hat work? It's their game, it's their rules. Yes, it does work. Does it work quickly? No. That's why people tend to want to cheat the system, and use the black hat tactics, so they can speed up the process while the white hat takes effect.

Google, as a search engine, earns their living by generating revenue through the sale of ads. They don't generate revenue by ranking your website at the very top of the page. They're very, very protective of that page, because, again, as we mentioned in a previous chapter, they want to deliver high quality content. They don't want to deliver crap to their users. They want to deliver a great user experience.

What does that mean for you as the website owner and entrepreneur? Well, following the advice of Google to optimize your website would be like asking a father, like Rob or myself, for advice on how best to seduce our daughters. We're just not going to do that. We're pretty protective of our daughters.

You need to find something, I like to say, in-between. Follow the guidelines, follow the concepts that Google uses, but if you're going to use some of the black hat tactics that are a little questionable, then protect and insulate yourself. This is what I refer to as the grey hat.

If you think about your site, it's in the very center of your business universe, and surrounding your site… and we'll cover this in more detail with the link building… you can put sites that, I like to call, too big to slap by Google. This would be sites like YouTube, which is owned by Google, Google Plus, Facebook, LinkedIn, Amazon and Apple to name just a few. You can generate links back to your site from these high value sites, and then at the same time you can interlink these with your content. Then you can then use the black hat tactics to increase the value of that insulated ring around your website.

If there's poor value going out to YouTube, you know what? They're not going to slap YouTube, Google just won't pass on the value to you. But if you pass on higher rankings to your video on YouTube, Google will pass it back to you.

This is what I would like to call grey hat. It's not really good, it's not really evil, it's kind of like everybody else in the world, somewhere in-between. You're using sound concepts, but you're doing it in such a way that if something should change in how Google puts out their algorithm, then it's not going to affect your site directly; it's going to go towards the insulating sites you have around you.

As I said, these insulating sites are too big to slap. They're not going to be delisted, they're not going to be devalued, they're not going to be dropped in the search rankings from Google, Yahoo or Bing; they're just too big to slap. Just like you've got banks out there that are too big to fail. These sites are too big to slap.

So what do you do if you followed some poor advice and find your site delisted?

If you find yourself getting delisted, the suggestion that I would make is: go out, clean up all the backlinks that are going to your site, clean up your content, remove the crap then essentially start from scratch as far as SEO goes. Start following some of the mostly white hat, little bit of grey, and stay away from anything that might get you into trouble.

Take your time, it does take a while. Again, if you

produce high quality content and you put it out on a consistent basis… and that content as we mention throughout this book should be relevant, recent, high quality, and of course unique… then you can find yourself moving yourself back up. It's going to take a while, so the best advice and suggestion I can give anybody, is if you want to take a shortcut ... don't.

What I find, is that if you follow the rules and follow the steps, you may not make it to the top right away. But, what I also find is if you do provide high quality content, every time there is an update and sites ahead of you that use questionable practices get delisted, or slapped, or pushed down, that automatically raises you up, and it gives you a very secure position.

Chapter 6

Backlinks & More

Not dead, nor too big to slap!

In this chapter we share the importance of backlinks. Some are good and some will down-right harm your website ranking. Maybe you've seen ads touting the viability of backlinks and how beneficial such links can have with ranking your website.

Let's go back a couple of years ago, when everybody wanted to get on that backlink bandwagon. You could get backlinks added to your site for *x* amount of dollars. The problem was that people were taking advantage of the loophole in the system. They were getting backlinks to everything to try to trick Google. It was like they were saying, "Hey you know I got all these backlinks."

Well, if you have an online web bookstore (or any store) and you want to sell product and increase your leverage on Google, you would go out and get all these back links pointed to your site. The problem with the whole scenario of linking everything to your site was that those back links weren't relevant. You had these websites, receiving backlinks from porn sites, from sports entertainment, associating with things that aren't relative or relevant to their site. Then after time Google decides,

"Hey you know what? We believe that you guys are taking advantage of the system so we're going to eliminate the value of your back links or eliminate the ones that we believe are not relevant your site."

The people that had all these irrelevant backlinks, were starting to see that their site was actually taking a hit and not showing up on searches anymore. They had all these backlinks that didn't belong. We've been telling people for years, if you're going to link with somebody, make sure that you're linking to people that share your common industry. That they're relevant to what you're doing and they actually increase the value of what you're delivering to others.

Initially, the idea behind the backlink is that if someone would link to your website or to your content the algorithm of a search engine was set up in such a way that that back link was considered a vote of confidence or vote of authority for your website. It's now become something that is abused and exploited to the point where it's not as effective anymore as it once was. Three years ago, two years ago even, some of the customers of ours still ranked well with irrelevant backlinks. And, sadly took the position that the one with the most backlinks wins.

Now, some would say backlinks are dead.

Not dead!

Not yet.

Backlinks are as valuable now, if not more so.

Sometimes it takes those trying to game the system for the system to be improved for those that follow the rules. One of the more powerful backlinks two years ago was to get a backlink from a University or EDU site. Well, that was just exploited all over the place to the point where having a back link to your site from a University has no power any longer.

What does work and what do you do now to create a back linking system for your website that wins?

There's a number of different things that you can do. One of the ways is a variation of what was once known as a link wheel. This is where people would create all these little mini sites that would be linked to one another like spokes on a wheel. They would link to other websites and create the impression of a bigger more dynamic system.

There's two problems with that. First, it became very obvious very quickly to the search engines that this was a link wheel or link network. They quickly got themselves shut down and blocked. The second problem, and this requires a little imagination...imagine a bucket of water, and you're pouring water inside the bucket. Now let's say all the incoming links to your website are actually the water going into your bucket. At the bottom of that bucket, you're going to be poking holes into it. If you have more water running out than you have coming in, you'll never fill that bucket. But if you have enough flow of water going into that bucket than you have going out, even though you have that leak, you will still fill up that bucket. That's the way it works with backlinks to a website. If you have more links going out than you have coming in then back linking isn't going to help you very much. With these link networks they have the links coming in but they have thousands of links going out.

Passing value on to user websites. The above scenario didn't do that. Yet, it can be done.

What you can do is create your own private link wheel. This is where you would go out and you would create your own content value outside your website. You can do this on video sharing sites like Vimeo, Daily Motion, YouTube. You can do this also for sites such as Facebook, Word Press, Blogger, Google Plus, Twitter and have these all linking back to your website and to one another and then have your content and links going into these sites. The reason we recommend these sites is they're too big to slap.

If you start sending trash into YouTube for example, backlinking a video from a porn site, (not that we would ever recommend that) Google is not going to penalize YouTube. It may not pass a whole lot of value back to you, but it's not going to penalize YouTube - it's their property.

It's the same thing with Facebook. It's too big to slap. Twitter, very much the same thing. Even Daily Motion and Vimeo are at the point now they're getting too big to slap, even though they are not a Google property.

If you were to build your own private link circle around your website it's going to give you two benefits. First, you're going to pass very valuable, relevant backlinks. Let's face it, if you have a website about dog training, then you set up dog training videos on YouTube, that's a relevant back link from having that dog training video on YouTube coming back to your site. Second, if you're going to be blogging about those dog training videos on blogger.com or wordpress.com, you are creating authority which gives elevates your website higher on search results. Some of the other things that people have also used and still use effectively today would be submitting and sharing articles.

Maybe you've heard about duplicate content being less effective or hurting your website. There's a difference though between duplicate content and syndication. If you take for example, at the time of this writing, we were just days away from when the first U.S

Ebola patient passed away in a Dallas hospital. If you did a Google search on 'US Ebola patient dies in Dallas hospital", you will see all the same news reports that have been syndicated out by the news wires to all these news outlets, newspapers and other media throughout the world all carrying the same content.

You'll also notice that whoever put it out first got the highest ranking. Anyone else that followed came in behind. When you syndicate content, it's the same thing. You can put out a piece of content somewhere and if it's the same, it may not help your ranking, but if it's relevant it will still count as a back link.

The danger with this though is you want to also make sure that it's relevant and unique. There are all kinds of products out there that will spread your content to make it pass as the same message but make it look and read differently or unique. Writing articles still works. The caveat here: it had better be a quality article. You don't want to be firing off a bunch of crap. We talked about getting slapped...well, if Google updates their algorithms, places you submit content to could get hurt and your backlinks disqualified. That happened to a number of article directories when it was discovered that the articles being submitted were less valuable than a pile of dog crap.

Many article sites have learned their lesson and are

a little bit pickier, a little bit more finicky now as to what they allow on their networks. Don't send out crap. You don't want your business represented with crap do you? Of course you don't.

Our recommendation is not to do something that we've seen people do time and time again. They would go out and create all these back links to their websites. However, these backlinks are all going to the homepage. Let's take dog training as an example.

If we are going to be talking about dog training and we are going to have an article on say, "House Training your dog," you would want to have a page on your website that talks about house training a dog and then link that article to that particular page. There is no sense bringing it up to the home page. The home page is going to get a lot of links. But, when you link deep inside your website you're going to increase the value of that particular page which, if you link that page to your home page, is going to lift it up as well. Articles still work but make it relevant, make it a high quality article, change your content a little bit and of course make it unique as you submit to other directories. Then link it back to the page on your site that that article is most relevant to.

Something else that we found that has still a lot of weight that still works, particularly when you become an authority in your field, is the opportunity to become a guest blogger. This is where you create your own content and you provide it to other blog owners. Most blogs are terribly neglected. A lot of blogs should be better maintained than they have been. That is one of the reasons why so many of these bloggers, particularly the high level bloggers, want fresh content to come in because it's very difficult to always maintain fresh new content on a regular basis. If you can develop a partnership in your field, you'll have lots of opportunities to share your knowledge, share your content and other blogs and like you back.

Is it an ideal way?

It depends on what your goals are and what you want your website to do. There are probably quicker, easier, simpler and faster ways to create quality back links to your website. Again, you're in the hands of somebody else so you're really relying on that somebody else to help your business. Which leads us to the next step and that is leaving comments on blogs. Now this was at one time a very effective means of ranking a website.

Paul had a website about six years ago for his multilevel marketing business. It had ranked very well on the front page of Google and one of the things that helped him was he was also very vocal on an industry blog run by a gentleman by the name of Troy Dooley. Paul was routinely commenting on Troy's blog and that would give him a relevant backlink because Paul was able to have his website address, his name and email on every comment. Within a short amount of time Paul noticed a spike of activity commenting on this blog and his MLM website moved up the search ranks.

Unfortunately a lot of people discovered this as well and they came up with automated tools that would go out and spam blog comments. There isn't a day that goes by that we go into a website that we manage and there is a spam comment somewhere that we are deleting and a spammer whose IP we're blocking.

Spamming blog type sites is still a tactic unscrupulous so-called SEO'ers push on unsuspecting website owners. Just the other day Rob was optimizing a designer built area rug cleaning site for a company out of New York and discovered 1300 comments...all spam. Not one legitimate comment. The website was only a month old too. Well, on the plus side, the website was constructed using Word Press and due to the features and plug-ins the spam comments were quickly eliminated. If you're going to have a website you need to be vigilant on who's leaving comments on your site.

Just a quick note about comment spam. One of Paul's first clients was a local artist that wanted a site as a gallery to display her work. This was early in his career and he made the mistake of looking for and downloading a free WordPress theme.

That was a mistake.

Free themes and plugins are notorious for attracting comment spam. This poor woman was getting comments linking to Chinese porn sites and Russian investment schemes. As soon as Paul changed the theme from a free theme to a theme he purchased from a reputable developer, the comment spam dropped considerably.

The other thing that we found that works very effectively is publishing your content. What do we mean by publish? Well, you can create a Kindle book. You can take the content that you create from a Google Hangout, Zoom, live cast or Skype, then strip off the audio and create an audio podcast. You can have it transcribed to create articles or more books.

Right now the most powerful search engine optimization that can you can create outside your website is to publish your content and publish it everywhere. Where are some of the places you can go?

We really like iTunes. Now you are creating a very valuable link coming to your website from Apple. Creating a Kindle book and having a link back to your websites from an author page on Amazon is a very powerful backlink. Having back links to your website from video sharing sites such as Vimeo, Daily motion and YouTube are very powerful backlinks to have to your websites.

Backlinks are still very valuable and a permanent way to increase the value of the rankings of your web page or the search engines. You have to do it right, you have to do it smart, you have to backlink to win so what that means is make sure that you're getting backlinks from a relevant site to your site and not from something that will be raising eyebrows or be a little shady.

Chapter 7

Misconceptions Challenged

Never hire Kevin Costner!

In 2011, Paul was running the marketing department for a local protective coatings company. It was a Line-X Franchise. When he started working with this company one of things that he was asked to do was to drive around and search out all the competition. He would get them give him a quote on a spray-on box liner for the pickup truck he was driving (in this case, the owner's pickup truck). It didn't take Paul very long to compile a list of all the local competitors... They were all listed up on the first two pages of Google.

Now, Paul went to work with this company with the idea that he was going to turn them into search engine bullies and used a lot of the tactics and tools that we're sharing in this book, and within six months Line-X of Winnipeg had owned the first fifteen pages of Google.

That's a hundred and fifty listings that we're talking about. Paul had secured his employer on just about every single one of them. The first competitor showed up on page seven, the second one showed up on page fifteen and there were a few directories and yellow page listings in between. Out of the hundred and fifty listings that was on the first fifteen pages of Google, Paul's employer owned about a hundred and thirty of them.

This is the concept we are talking about, taking the idea of becoming a search engine bully, of pushing everybody off the front page, to an extreme level. Now, that was 2011 and if you do a search on the phrase, **"*Winnipeg spray-on box liners*"** you'll still see a lot of what Paul did on page one. Their website will still be on page one, a video that was made in May 2011 will still be on page one.

Everything else has kind of crept down or disappeared and has been replaced by the competitors that have created and put up new, relevant content, including one of the first clients that Paul had after he left the franchise and that was for the competition.

Now, there's two things we want to share with this story.

One is that because the Line-X franchise owned the first fifteen pages with, it took Paul six months to crack that for the competition. Paul decided at that point he's never going to go into competition with himself again. Secondly, when you're not putting up constant and fresh content, you will get replaced by those people that do.

The point of this story is simply this: had Paul stayed and continued to put up the content, his employer would still be dominating the search engines and the competition definitely wouldn't have a chance.

Unlike the Ronco Oven, it's not set it and forget it. You need to continue working on it. SEO is not a sprint, it's a marathon. Yes, you'll rank for some keywords very quickly and the keywords you want to rank for are going to take some time, but if you continue following the best practices we're outlining in this book and continue to publish and syndicate content, then you'll find that you will get the results that you're looking for and you will insulate yourself from the efforts of your competition trying to catch up.

One of the misconceptions we hear every day, from people coming to us, "Well, the web company says it's going to take six to nine months for my site to show up" and we just shake our heads, because we know that's just not true. Yes, for certain keywords, for certain key phrases, we can probably have you on page one of Google within a few days. Once you're on page one, there are steps that you need to take to stay there.

You need to keep submitting articles, you need to keep your blog going, you need to do all these things that we suggest in this book.

If you cannot do that, you will slowly fall back down the ranks and then you're going to come back and say, "*I need you to put me back on page one.*"

And we'll reply like we always do, "*Are you going to follow these rules?*"

If your reply is "*No*" or "*Maybe*", we will come back with, "*Well, then there's nothing we can do, because it's just going to yo-yo back and forth.*"

Look, do you honestly want to wait nine months for your site to get out there, like the web people are telling you? Or do you want to have immediate success?

Success comes from following a plan. Based on what we're showing you in this book, if you want to be successful with your website, with the internet marketing, there are rules that you have to follow.

You can't set it and forget it. You have to do the work! You can't rely on nine months of waiting. By the time your competitors are waiting nine months, you could've already dominated page one, page two, page three and have success be part of your daily routine.

Here's the flaw with that nine month timeline...

By the time you get everything you need to stay optimized for that keyword, in nine months, the search engines are going to change their algorithm. Yep, they change the rules and then what you did for those last nine months may or may not be effective anymore. Now you're back to the drawing board. Ready to invest in another nine month plan?

Rather than trying to focus on that type of thing, follow the best practices that we're outlining and do so consistently. That's key. Relevant consistency is what's going to help you win this race and it's not a slow and steady thing. Yes, you can get things up on the first page in days.

In the used car market Paul had a client that was a dealer. Paul got him on the first page for the keyword "***sub-prime auto loans***" within two days and that was just by sending out a press release and implementing the power of Google+.

Now, is that a high value keyword? Not really. It's more of an industry term (see the chapter "Go **APE**). It actually took Paul six months to get ranked for "used car financing" because it's a *very* competitive market. That's something you're going to have to actually weigh into your strategy: how competitive is the market you're in?

Most entrepreneurs are one man operations fighting against large, multi-million dollar companies that have SEO teams. These big companies are investing tens of thousands of dollars a month into being positioned at the top of page one...and they have a head start over you.

One or two word generic or branded keywords are going to take you way too long to try to dominate.

Natural key phrases that illicit a deeper meaning or contain type of product or service and location will be more effective at ranking.

Patience, grasshopper.

It can take a while.

And, that's the reason that you need to realize that for some of the low-hanging fruit keywords, it's very quick and easy to get ranked on the front page of Google. If you're in a market with competitive keywords, you're not going to get ranked in a day or two. Nor in a week...maybe not even in a month.

Don't set it and forget it.

Follow the best practices outlined in this book on a consistent basis, and keep doing it.

We realize this sounds like a great way for guys like Rob and Paul to sell continuity programs and it is, we'll be the first ones to admit that, but you have to benefit from those continuity programs; if you don't then there's no point. Make sure you're getting results, track the results, be in this for the long-haul and you will be rewarded.

There are so many sites that we see that don't have a blog. Ugh!

Paying big bucks for a site and only making it a static representation of what you do without any way of educating and entertaining clients or providing them with relevant content that makes you the authority is big waste of money.

Look, if you want to see a billboard, just drive down a highway; you don't need that on your website. You need something that's more interactive, more content-delivered. If you want your web site to work, then you have to put a little work into it.

Kevin Costner is not building your site!

"Build it and they will come." doesn't work with websites.

EVER!

Put the time and effort into it! Get the content syndicated!

And in the words of Larry the Cable Guy, "**Get'er Done!**"

Chapter 8

SEO Deconstructed

Things that begin with 'H'

We get calls all the time from entrepreneurs desperate to get their websites seen on Google and the many other search engines. It's sad really...they've spent thousands of dollars on the layout and content of the site only to have it seen by a few.

Then they get sucked into running Adwords, Facebook ads and various Pay Per Click campaigns only to realize more money is being flushed down the proverbial drain.

So, they come to us already beaten down and distrusting of what we can do for them. They've heard the promises before and so now we have to spend time educating them as to why their web guy screwed up.

They just don't understand why people can't just type their name or their company name into Google to find them. And, they cringe when we tell them their name is irrelevant to Google searches. Unless said customer actually knows the exact spelling of your name or product, the chances of them finding you are slim to none.

So here we are writing a book to try to explain to people once again why they need proper SEO for their websites. And why, the same keywords and phrases should never be used to describe each page of your website.

Every website that's created has (or should have) what's called Meta coding. It's this coding that Google and the other search engines use to index your site in their ranking system. No meta coding or lousy coding and your site is stuck in the phantom zone. That's any page that isn't Page 1 of Google, Bing, Yahoo or any the search engine you frequent the most. If you're not on Page 1 then forget it...because rarely do people look beyond that page when searching.

Now to the actual fundamentals...

Meta coding is broken into 3 sections:

(1) Title

(2) Description and

(3) Keywords.

The **Meta Title** is what shows up in or above your search bar depending what browser you use...its function is to give a brief synopsis of your page in 60 characters or less. I usually tell clients pick 2 or 3 keywords that best describe the page plus whatever cities you service to give the search bots (a term used to describe the way search engines file your site in their system) a better understanding of what you do.

Next is the **Meta Description**. This is a short paragraph limited to no more than 160 characters that expand on the keywords you used in your Title. This information again should reflect what's on the actual webpage.

Now we get to **Meta Keywords**...and this where most people get confused. Meta Keywords are the words that reflect what the page is about nothing more. This is where 99% of web designers make their mistakes. They stuff keywords. They put keywords in that have nothing to do with the page or what they do. Limit your keywords to no more than 15, this keeps each page unique and prevents overuse of redundant words.

Here's the caveat...Google doesn't even use the Meta Keywords in your coding...so stuffing them doesn't do any good. Sure the other search engines do...but, if you stick to relevant words your chances of ranking higher are so much better.

So why do we share this great information and potentially give away our secrets?

Well, frankly we're tired of the so-called web companies not knowing how to use SEO correctly and driving everyone to spend gobs of money on AdWords.

Do you realize Google invented AdWords to fill a void and help websites get seen?

Yep, they realized web designers weren't coding sites correctly so they created a product that took advantage of those who got screwed the first time. And now they continue to get screwed with every AdWords campaign. Ingenious or unscrupulous?

We'll leave that question for another time and maybe for a future book.

Now let's focus on...

Simplicity and "H" tags.

"H" tags (or header tags) are a way to give headlines and descriptions to your work. The higher the "H" tag the lower the importance of the header.

You have your Main title, you have your subhead, you even have key points. Now, the mistake we see a lot of people make, is using the "H" tags the wrong way These tags typically tends to be bigger in font size, bolder and maybe italicized depending on how they are set up. Instead of using a proper HTML code to increase the fonts size of a phrase or bolded out to italicize it, people will put the content they want to enhance inside these tags. You should have just one H1 tag on your page.

You should have maybe two or three H2 tags on your page. Now if you need to make something bigger or bolder or a different font then instead of using the H tags and title tags make the changes in either the cascading style sheet or do some on-page styling in the header part of your page or even some in-line styling just to make a change to that particular phrase or thought section.

Using proper and accurate HTML code is very important to ranking your page. If you over do the title tags you're actually going to hurt yourself rather than help yourself.

Sorry...we went a bit geeky there!

Now on to the simplicity part.

Web designers like to create brilliant works of art and there's nothing wrong with that but, they tend to turn over the content writing to some over qualified English Literature major. Then we get these websites that read like novels trying desperately to pull us into the story. UGH!

Sure, we love a good story. But, not from a website that we're trying to determine if they provide the solution to our needs.

If keywords are King and content is Queen, then

make the Queen a dignitary who is there to intrigue but not bore her audience.

In Google's latest smelly animal updated algorithm, content seems to be the thing web designers are yapping about. More content...we need more content.

Content written for the sake of Google is a terrible, horrible, down-right wrong way of ranking your website. The reality is, if all you have to say falls in the realm of 150 words then so be it. "But my web designer said I need 1000 words minimum!" You don't. Call "B.S." and move on.

Content that is boring will turn off your audience and lead to zero sales.

Bottom line...simplicity with content, proper "H" tagging and mastering Meta coding will give you SEO powers.

Chapter 9

Optimizing YouTube

Stumble, stutter, and close your eyes!

YouTube was one of those fun things that when it came out in 2005, was created to allow people to share short video clips with one another. Nobody at that time knew it was going to grow to become the monster that it is. Right now YouTube is the second largest search engine on the web. That's actually one of the other big reasons why you'd want to optimize YouTube.

Up until now we've been focusing a lot on Google. Rightfully so, since Google is the 800 pound gorilla as far as search engines. Oh, but YouTube...just happens to be the second largest search engine on the web. And incidentally owned by Google.

We hear people tell us if they need something, they go to Google. But when they need to know *how to do* something, they go to YouTube.

Paul has a client, who owns a used car dealership. And of course, this dealership has a service department. The manager of the service department insists that anytime they do work on vehicles even though they might know how to do the work, they always look it up on YouTube first.

The manager does this for two reasons: (1) it's going to bring it top of mind to his technicians and (2) someone may have figured out a faster, easier, cheaper and better way to get the job done.

Now can you see why YouTube is such a huge, powerful weapon to add to your arsenal.

It's all about engagement!

The problem we see is that a lot of the videos that are out there now do very little to engage traffic to their respective websites. And that lack of engagement does little to build authority.

One of the topics Rob covers in his book "*Share: 27 Ways to Boost Your Social Media Experience, Build Trust and Attract Followers*" is all about creating videos that generate engagement, create authority and build trust.

Here's the breakdown to make engaging videos...in 4 easy to follow steps.

1. **Pose a Question**
2. **Introduce Yourself**
3. **Answer The Question**
4. **Tell People How To Contact You**

Every video is an answer to a single question. And to keep people hooked on your videos and not bore them to death, make them under 5 minutes in length, preferably about 2 to 3 minutes. In a short time you could easily have hundreds of videos working 24/7 as your search engine salesman, educating consumers on everything there is to know about your service.

What questions?

When clients ask us what kind of questions should they answer in their videos, we respond by telling them that's actually one of the easiest things to do.

Take for example...

When someone gives you a call on the phone or comes into your business, I'm sure they have a lot of questions that you get asked frequently besides, "How much do you charge?"

In fact, it's those questions that get asked repeatedly that will help you get started making your educational videos. Why repeat the same answers over and over when you can automate the process with a series of videos.

Then move on from there with questions you wish clients would ask.

Keep a running list of questions so you always have pool to draw from. Easy-peasy.

Uploading Your Video...the fun part!

Okay, the actual part of uploading is sometimes monotonous and boring...but the really fun part comes from keywording your videos for maximum searchability.

While you are waiting for your video to upload you can start the process of describing what the video is all about and how it's a benefit to consumers.

First, start by putting some type of link on your video back to either your website, your fan page, another video, somewhere where it gets people to engage you further down the road. Secondly, transcribe that video and put that transcription as part of the description, or you simply put a summary description and let people know exactly what that video is about.

Next, we would encourage anyone doing a video to make the title of the video very similar to what you're talking about on the video, that becomes the dominant key word in the title.

YouTube is going to suggest keywords based on your transcription or your summary. Use some of them, but also use some of your own keywords to help ranking that video to where you want it to go.

Ranking your videos...using YouTube's Technology!

The content of the video, the spoken word, isn't something that's going to be ranked as far as keywords. But, your captioning on those videos... now that's another story. YouTube offers closed-captioning for the hearing impaired and this is one way to gain an advantage. Another way is with transcription. YouTube will transcribe your video...well, sort of.

It's really quite humorous when you read what their transcription service offers you. Actually, humorous is being kind. To be blunt...their transcription really sucks. It stinks. It takes a while, but it is to your benefit to take that audio file, send it off to someone to transcribe, and then fix the closed-caption. It does take a bit of time, but you're going to get a higher ranking on the search engines because of it.

Same things with annotations. You can now link to outside pages on the annotations throughout the video. You can put a call to action on that video, where someone would click on that call to action and take them to your website.

Don't be afraid to take advantage of some of the tools to optimize the video on YouTube. Basically in a nutshell, what we recommend and what we have people follow is you start off by using a key word based title as your mantra. Make it as close to the subject at hand as possible, and at the same time make sure it has key words you want to optimize for.

Link the video to the landing page that you're discussing in it. A good example is when Paul was setting up a bunch of videos for a local salon, and had them talk about what makes the facials they give their customers the best in the city, he would link the video to the facials page, not the home page.

If you can link the content of your video to a specific page in your website and do what we call "deep linking," by all means, deep link it. Put key words in the description, or actually use the transcript in the description, and then put the link, back into the video where you want people to go.

Fix and edit the captions on your video.

Here's something Paul stumbled on, and after many experiments discovered this simple trick works wonders at ranking not only your video but also your website. Here's how...

First list your website link to your YouTube video then put that video link on the webpage your link mentions in the video itself. Two things will happen.

You can get the video itself on YouTube to rank, then you can get that video page on your website to rank. Now, by doing that, you get two listings on the front page of Google instead of just the one. It just squeezes people out, this turns you into search engine bully.

The reason you make multiple videos is that more is always better. Never stop at one. Paul did a demo a couple years ago for a carpet cleaner in Flint, Michigan, one video is still on page 1 at the time of this book writing, yet the second video he did, no idea where it is. One or two videos, it's hit or miss depending on how well you optimize it, but when you get ten out there, or even twenty or thirty or a hundred, you become the authority in your niche.

Being the Authority!

One of Rob's clients is a medical malpractice attorney in New York, who now has 1500 videos on YouTube. Yeah, you read that right, 1500. The videos are based on questions gleaned from various past cases, from his clients and his own observations. What's cool is sometimes he'll change the question so it's very similar to one he just did, but distinctly different when he gives the answer.

It's all these videos that help him not only get cases, but make him the authority in New York. He's top of mind on Google and on YouTube. People are finding him, and they just love his videos. He doesn't have to do any other type of advertising whatsoever.

One of the best case studies ever would be the story

of Gary Vaynerchuk. He is a consultant who just finished writing a social media marketing book not too long ago called, "Jab, Jab, Jab, Right Hook,".

Gary's start with YouTube was trying to save his family's wine store business and he wanted to increase sales of bottles of wine. What did he do? He had a weekly show that he published and syndicated on YouTube, and he was educating people about the different types of wines. Where you would serve it, how you would serve it. His original videos were really crude, and of course as he got better at it they got a little bit more slick and a lot more professional looking.

That's the key thing here, is people are not looking for actors, they're looking for you. They want a real person to do business with. An actor is going to be perfect. You and I, we're human, we're fallible, we're going to make mistakes, we're going to stumble, we're going to stutter, we're going to go, "Oh wow," we're going to make mistakes like closing our eyes when we talk. That's fine. Be yourself. Be authentic, and create your celebrity with it.

Be Real...Be Human...Be Fallible!

Chapter 10

Getting on Page 1

Becoming the search engine bully!

Finally, yes, we get to the chapter that answers the proverbial question of "How Do I Get On Page 1?" And, if you've been paying attention throughout chapters 1-9, you should have an idea of not only the keywords to use, but how to write the content to attract the right clients into your funnel.

Now we take it a step further.

Social Proof!

Well, one of the things that we believe everybody should be doing, and not because Rob has written many books on social media, but because YOU SHOULD BE using social media to help bring all those fans, friends and followers into your funnel to get them to help you distribute your links, messages and website to their friends and fans.

One of the things that I believe is very important to help boost your ranks is utilizing the big 7; Facebook, Twitter, LinkedIn, Google+, Instagram, Pinterest, and YouTube.

Now we covered YouTube, but we really haven't

gotten into any of the social proof, the social influence, the social media as if...they really call it, it's not really media. It's basically social equity. You're building your relationship with somebody else using these platforms.

All of the social proof networks out there will do a lot to boost your credibility. They'll create your trust factor as the authority in what you do, but they also will build up your backlinks, which is something that we spoke about in previous chapters, but we're going to also mention it a little bit here. You have good backlinks and you have bad backlinks. Social proof gives you the good back links that you need to help build up what Google is going to give you as the authority. The more of those positive reinforcement backlinks that you have, the better.

Let's face it, Facebook, Twitter, LinkedIn, Google+, Instagram, Pinterest and YouTube, these are sites that are too big to get slapped or barred by Google. You're not going to do any damage to yourself now or in the future by creating back links from these big 7 social sites. Make sure you use them to your favor. The really cool thing is, on Pinterest, you can actually syndicate your videos there.

Submit, Submit, Submit!

As Paul and I were developing the concept for this book, we did a dozen or so Google Hangouts, to which we generated transcripts, video and audio files. These various elements were used to create articles, press releases and content for various blogs and audio programs.

Whether or not you'll be taking content off of a video that you produced or made with someone else, you use that content in such a way that you could actually produce articles to use to submit to media sites. Now you're going to generate not only back links from that, but it builds upon that authority that you're trying to create.

One thing that we have found that's been very, very powerful in addition to article submissions is to submit a press release. This is something that after creating your website, we highly recommend you do. Whether it be a re-release on the site that you've repaired, or a brand new site, or something new, creating a press release and submitting it to the various press directories that are out there may or may not get you any press, or even an article written about you. But it is a very good solid link back to your site. Take it from Paul...on several occasions he's had the press release that he's submitted on behalf of a client rank on page 1 and stay there for a very long time.

Okay, there's two benefits to submitting a press release. Would you like to know what they are? Of course you would.

One, when you have a press release sitting on page 1, that's a piece of real estate on the first page of the search engines that your competition's not sitting at. Two, if someone reads the press release, your link to your site is usually in that press release, so they can follow that to your website so you get traffic from that, and hopefully if everything's done right, new business. At the same time, it kicks up the value of the backlinks to your site. If you can get your site and the press release on that same page on the front of Google, then you're on your way to becoming a search engine bully.

Absolutely!

Add in fresh content and blam-o!

If nothing else, you've got 12 months of the year, you've got about 15 different holidays every year. Run a special. As we are wrapping up this book Paul just finished Thanksgiving in Canada, then we have Halloween coming up. We've got Thanksgiving coming up in the United States. In Canada we have Remembrance Day, in the United States we have Veteran's Day. We have Black Friday, Cyber Monday, we have Christmas, we have New year's, we have President's Day, we have all kinds of different sports events that are coming up.

Gray Cup in Canada, Super Bowl in the United

States if you're not into real football. (Ha-ha, those Canadians are so funny.) We have Family Day here in Canada in February, we have Easter, we have Good Friday, we have spring, we have winter, we have fall, we have summer, we have Canada Day, 4th of July, Victoria Day, Memorial Day, there's just so many different holidays that you can key a promotion or special around, and just come up with something new and fresh.

I'm not saying give away everything or offer discounts and train your customers to buy at a discount. I'm saying come up with a new promotion or offer for each of these holidays and special events. Create the events, and keep something fresh on your website as a result. I find that the websites that get the most traffic are the websites that are always coming up with new and better reasons to come back.

Whether it's a new video that you put up on YouTube, and you shared on Facebook, Twitter, and various social networks, or a blog post offering more tips...it adds to your authority, credibility and backlinks.

Oh yeah, blogs...let's talk about them.

Don't forget your blogs! We see a lot of great websites, but they don't keep their blogs up to date. When we look at their site and it says "Visit our blog" and after we click on it says the last blog post was

2011...there's a sign! That tells me that you don't really care, and you're not keeping things fresh and up to date.

Here's a tip: Even if you're not interested in blogging, post at least one blog entry a month. It just tells your customers that you care enough that you want to spend the time to educate them on why they need to use your service. And, it tells the search engines your site is being maintained with fresh, relevant content.

Here's another tip: Make sure you keep your copyrights up to date. Oh yeah, it's a big deal. Most websites have a date stamp or published date of when the site was created or last edited. Keeping the date current may not sound like an important factor but to your visitors and to the search engines it could be the difference between fresh and stale bread. And, trust me there is a difference.

We've seen dates on sites copyrighted as far back as 2008. And, a website that hasn't been updated in that many years means it most likely was abandoned by its owners. And, honestly lots of things have changed in that time, both technologically and socially. Websites have come a long way in educating, entertaining and engaging visitors. Keep your website copyright current for the year and keep the content updated.

One last tip: Proper grammar and punctuation now

are a key factor in getting you ranked.

Oh, boy is that right!

"Write like you speak, and talk from your heart."

If English is your primary language, but you weren't such a great English student in high school, then get someone to proofread your site. Make sure there's no typos, spelling mistakes, or grammatical errors. It counts. Hire an proofreader. Check your work. Proofread it again. It's a simple little thing that'll return huge rewards for you. (Hmm, I wonder how many mistakes are in this book. If you find some tell us, we want to know.)

In summary...getting onto page 1.

Simple as giving social proof and establishing yourself as an authority. We've got the 7 big websites, and that's Facebook, Twitter, LinkedIn, Google+, Instagram, Pinterest and YouTube. Keep things fresh and up to date with articles and blog posts. Feel free to submit to article directories and even share these articles or posts on social networks. Optimize your pages. We've talked about this before, but part of page optimization's going to be correct spelling, correct grammar, no typos, as well as accurate keywords in the title and description. Make sure you Go **APE** as we've discussed in the previous chapter.

Make sure there's no dead links coming into or out of your website. If there's a link coming into your website that's no longer valid, you know what? Eliminate it. If there's a link going out of your website that's going to a 404 page, get rid of it. If you have a page that you've eliminated on your website, but you still have links to that page floating around in cyber land, eliminate those links.

Increase your backlinks. This is something that as an ongoing SEO practice, you want to continue to do. You want to continue to go out and build your social authority as well as your authority in your niche. Keep your content fresh and interesting, timely and up to date, and don't be afraid to let people know about it, so submit your press releases.

Almost The End

Paul and I would like to thank you for allowing us into your life and giving us the opportunity to show you how easy search engine optimization can be with the right instruction.

We would love for you to share this book with your friends, family, colleges, your boss and whomever might benefit from it.

We would also like to ask you a favor...

If you liked this book would you take a picture with it and share with us on Facebook. Please tag us in your picture.

https://www.facebook.com/RobAnspach

https://www.facebook.com/TheIndustryGiant

Oh, and please leave a 5 star review on Amazon and Barnes & Noble. This lets others know what you think and helps them decide if this book is worth the read.

www.amazon.com

www.bn.com

Frequently Asked Questions

What's the difference between "on-page" and "off-page" SEO? "On-Page" SEO is the optimization that is done to your website. "Off-Page" SEO consists of anything done to promote your website from outside resources that point back to your website.

Should I get a domain that is keyworded to my industry? No, not necessarily! That was "old-school" thinking and it worked for a time. But is not required and actually we don't recommend it. Companies were buying up every variation of their name or service in domains and going broke and frustrated maintaining those domains. Keep it simple. With proper optimization you only need one domain to worry about.

What pages of my site get indexed? That's entirely up to you. You want to have at least your main pages indexed. If you have a shopping cart or e-commerce store of sorts some components don't need to be indexed. If you have pages that are designed for private viewing then you shouldn't have those indexed either. Indexing makes your pages available for search and makes it easier for people to find you.

How long does it typically take to see results from SEO? Results vary from person to person and the experience they bring to the table. But if your web person tells you it could take 6-9 months for results, go get a second opinion. Paul and Rob have seen keywords rank in as little as a few hours, and one plumber in Arizona Rob worked with received a $6500 order 3 days after his site was optimized. It all depends on how the site is optimized and who did the work.

Can I do the SEO myself? Sure! But we wouldn't recommend it. There are certain aspects that look easy or "doable" but without the proper understanding of coding or proper placement of keywords the money you save trying to do yourself may end up costing you more in the long run. Same goes with hiring the teenage nerd down the street or the out of work cousin who thinks he knows computers.

Why didn't my last SEO person make changes to my site? Most SEO companies focus on "Off-Page" SEO which takes times and costs big bucks. It's an easy payday for those companies because they have their systems automatically programmed to send out your information on a monthly basis. Takes them minutes and costs unsuspecting website owners hundreds if not thousands every month. And sadly, doesn't do anything for ranking. By following the advice in this book you'll have the knowledge to bypass those bogus companies and start getting your site ranked with "On-Page" SEO followed by the right way to do "Off-Page" SEO.

Why isn't my page ranking? Well, first let's check the meta tags, then the content and then determine if you have any backlinks. Do you have a blog? Are social share buttons on your site so others can share your content? In most cases we find that your website is lacking a combination of things that, if implemented, would help rank your site higher on search results.

Does blogging really help? It goes back to relevant content. If all you are doing is pushing a nonsensical post out every day just to blog, then NO, it won't work. But, if you write relevant content and do so to educate your audience then it becomes a benefit and not an unwelcomed piece of rubbish nobody wants. If you're not so good with writing then hire someone to write your post, but make sure it's original, non-duplicated, relevant content.

I heard social media is all you really need nowadays is that true? Your website brings people into your funnel, your social media networks keep people in that funnel. Social media combined with your web presence helps consumers make inform choices and engage in what you are sharing. If you optimize your website for better search ranking and you engage fans through your social networking then you will have a combination that will ensure success.

I've gone through 3 SEO companies in 2 years and none could rank my website what did they do wrong?
We hear this a lot. And, it goes back to Question # 6. Most likely they used "Off-Page" SEO techniques that didn't stick. Or they have no idea what keywords and content you should have to rank your website. Since no one has ever heard the acronym "**A.P.E.**" before pertaining to the thinking behind optimizing websites that would probably be the reason most SEO companies can't rank sites well.

Glossary Of SEO Terms

404 Error Code – means the webpage you are trying to find is no longer available.

Algorithm - in search terms means a way for certain data to be processed to give the best results in a faster way.

Backlink – are also called incoming links or inbound links, they are essentially links that point back to a website or web page.

Black Hat – are aggressive tactics that don't follow search engine protocols.

Blacklist – is when search engines refuse to list your website, usually caused by Black Hat tactics.

Bulletin Board – a precursor to social networking allows people to communicate and share audio/video data.

Forum – is similar in nature to a bulletin board but is more structured and designed more as a "one question" per topic and not as free flowing as today's social networks.

Google – the world's largest search engine.

Google Trends – a simple way to access additional data or keywords based on "real time" information.

Gray Hat – not necessarily aggressive SEO tactics but not really industry protocol either.

H Tag – (or header tags) are a way to give headlines and descriptions to your work. The higher the "H" tag the lower the importance of the header.

HTML – stands for Hyper Text Markup Language and is a standardized system that makes text, font, color, graphics and hyperlinks work more effectively on the web.

Link Wheel – is a way to link several sites together through backlinks then point them to a site which acts as the receiver or hub.

Meta Description – is a short paragraph limited to no more than 160 characters that expand on the keywords you used in your Title.

Meta Keywords – are the words that reflect what the page is about nothing more.

Meta Title – is what shows up in or above your search bar depending what browser you use...its function is to give a brief synopsis of your page in 60 characters or less.

Optimize – to make the keywords and content on a website more effective to attract the right audience and rank higher on search results.

Plug In – is a widget program that enables Word Press sites to do more.

Ranking – term used to give an idea where on search engines a website shows up.

SEO – is anything you can do to get your website to rank higher on the various search engines for the keywords and content that reflect your industry.

Template Site – a inexpensive way to build a website that typically doesn't require coding skills, yet rarely offers the SEO support needed to get the site ranked on the search engines.

Watermark – a way to place an image or text on a photo to protect against theft.

White Hat – the best way to optimize a website and have it rank on the search engines. Follow the rules and stay safe.

Word Press – a customizable utility website that can be adapted with all the bells and whistles needed to not only rank on the search engines but impress your customers.

YouTube – the industry giant for video hosting.

Resources

This page is more a reference so you know where to go and what to use to help you improve your SEO and internet marketing abilities.

If using Word Press here are a few plug-ins we recommend:

- All In One SEO – for optimizing your Meta content
- Rotating Text – awesome for testimonials
- Social Media Widget – social share buttons
- Akismet –eliminating spam
- DIVI – integrated full featured theme
- Author Bio Box – displays author's info below blog posts
- Google Analytics – displays real time statistics
- Scheduled Post Trigger – keeps blogs posted when scheduled
- SumoMe – helps automate your engagement
- WooCommerce – makes selling products easier
- WP SEO Structured Data Schema – helps expand on the information you want the search engines to know about your business, organization, blog posts, ratings and more.

If you're sick and tired of your hosting company or they aren't providing the service you need (backups, security against hackers, updates, SSL encryption, etc.) we have a solution that we're confident will work for you. To learn more contact Paul today.

Paul@TitanMarketingSolutions.com

Connecting With The Authors

Rob Anspach a former carpet cleaner turned Global Social Media Strategist, SEO Expert, Author and Speaker. Rob took the experiences learned owning a cleaning company for 20 years to first establish himself as a teacher to cleaners then an authority to entrepreneurs and corporations worldwide. Rob as authored, coauthored or produced many books, articles and resources to help entrepreneurs across the globe.

You can follow Rob on Facebook, LinkedIn, YouTube and Twitter.

To connect with Rob use the URL below.

https://AnspachMedia.com

Paul Douglas also spent time as a carpet cleaner before becoming a search engine bully. Paul honed his skills as a direct response copywriter, marketer and internet fanatic. It was these skills that clients trusted that enable Paul to become Winnipeg's most sought after SEO expert. In 2012 Paul launched Titan Marketing Solutions with the goal of helping all his clients get found on every online platform, desktop, laptop and every connected pocket device.

You can follow Paul on Facebook, LinkedIn and YouTube.

To connect with Paul use the URL below.

https://TitanMarketingSolutions.com

Coaching / Speaking Programs

If you'd like to expand on what you've learned here in this book may we suggest our Intermediate and Advanced courses. These are designed to take you to the next level and enhance your internet marketing skill set and give you the powers of a true SEO Bully.

Or hiring us to speak at your next event, conference or training session.

Intermediate Course

This is a 10 week course that covers in more detail every chapter of this book with step-by-step instruction. Facilitated by both Paul and Rob, using Zoom, Skype or other online technologies, participants get to interact with the authors in real time and discover from the masters the intricacies of optimization.

Advanced Course

This is a 3 day intensive class that is offered only to those who have completed the Intermediate Course. This advanced class completes your training and makes you a Certified Search Engine Bully. The Advanced Courses will take place in the USA or Canada depending on time of year.

For more information on the courses or to arrange speaking contact

Rob at info@anspachmedia.com

Paul at Paul@titanmarketingsolutions.com

SEO Critique Special Offer

Here's what you do... if you believe that your website could use help whereas it's…

not ranking where you had hoped,

not bringing in the sales,

not generating the followers...

it's time you contact us.

We'll look over your website and if it's a candidate for improvement we'll let you know. We'll share with you all the places fixes should occur to rank higher.

 You can either try doing it yourself (not recommended) or hire us.

Contact us today to get started.

Rob Anspach at Anspach Media (United States)
https://AnspachMedia.com

Paul Douglas at Titan Marketing Solutions (Canada)
https://TitanMarketingSolutions.com

Other Books By Rob Anspach

Books Produced By Paul Douglas

Books can be ordered directly from Amazon.

Share this book!

I mean it!

Tell your friends all about this book.

Share where you bought it.

Share it at lunch!

Share it at the gym!

Share it on the beach!

Share it on social media.

Share it using these hashtags…

#OptimizeThis

Made in the USA
Middletown, DE
15 May 2019